Steadwell Books World Tour

SOUTH AFRICA

TONYA LESLIE

Steadwell Books

Raintree Steck-Vaughn Publishers

Harcourt Company

Austin New York
www.steck-vaughn.com

Published by Raintree Steck-Vaughn Publishers,
an imprint of Steck-Vaughn Company.

Editor: Simone T. Ribke
Designer: Maria E. Torres

Library of Congress Cataloging-in-Publication Data
Leslie, Tonya.
    South Africa / by Tonya Leslie.
      p. cm. -- (Steadwell books world tour)
    Summary: Describes the history, geography, economy, government, religious and social
life, various famous people, and outstanding tourist sites of South Africa. Includes a recipe
for Mealie-meal, a steamed porridge.
    Includes bibliographical references and index.
    ISBN 0-7398-5756-8
    1. South Africa--Juvenile literature. [1. South Africa.] I. Title. II. Series.

DT1719 .L47 2002
916.8--dc21   2002017866

Printed in the United States of America
1 2 3 4 5 6 7 8 9 10 WZ 07 06 05 04 03 02

Photo acknowledgments
Cover-a ©Steve Vidler/SuperStock; cover-b ©Mark Downey/The Viesti Collection; cover-c
©Frans Lanting/Minden Pictures; cover-d ©Vladpans/eStock Photography; p.1b ©Mark
Downey/The Viesti Collection; p.1c ©Wendy Stone/Odyssey Productions; p.3a ©Mark
Downey/The Viesti Collection; p.3b ©Wendy Stone/Odyssey Productions; p.5 ©James D.
Watt/Visuals Unlimited; p.7 ©Guy Stubbs/ CORBIS; p.8 ©Charles O'Rear/CORBIS; p.13a
©Michael Fogden/DRK Photo; p.13b ©Vladpans/ eStock Photography; p.14 ©Paul
Souders/Worldfoto; p.15 ©Frans Lanting/Minden Pictures; p.16 ©Steve Vidler/ SuperStock;
p.19 ©Walter Bibikow/The Viesti Collection; p.21 ©Theo Allofs/Getty Images; p.23 ©George
Lepp/Getty Images; p.24 ©Jason Lauré; p.25 ©Dave G. Houser/CORBIS; p.27 ©Robert
Frerck/ Odyssey Productions; p.28 ©Serge Attal/TimePix; p.29 ©SuperStock; p.31a ©Jim
Brandenburg/Minden Pictures; p.31b ©Ghislain & Marie David de Lossy/Getty Images; p.33
©Luc Hosten/CORBIS; p.34 ©Jason Lauré; p.35 ©Ulrike Holsten/StockFood; p.37 ©Walter
Bibikow/The Viesti Collection; p.38 ©Bob Krist/eStock Photography; p.39 ©Anthony
Bannister/CORBIS; p.40 ©Joe Viesti/The Viesti Collection; p.41 ©Walter Bibikow/The Viesti
Collection; p.42 ©Steve Vidler/SuperStock; p.43b ©Wendy Stone/Odyssey Productions;
p.43c ©M. Crame/Christine Osborne Pictures; p.44a ©Bettmann/ CORBIS; p.44b ©Yoav
Lemmer/ CORBIS; p.44c ©AP/Wide World.

Additional photography by Getty Royalty Free and Map Resources.

CONTENTS

Welcome to South Africa

Are you interested in seeing wild animals? How would you like to meet and greet a Zulu warrior? Would you like to go shark watching? If so, South Africa is the place for you! Whether you are actually heading out to South Africa or just taking a trip there in your mind, this book offers you a glimpse into this country's history, land, and people. So let's travel together to see South Africa.

A Tip as You Get Started

- *Use the Table of Contents*

Do you already know what you are looking for? Maybe you just want to know what topics this book will cover. The Contents page tells you what topics you will read about. It tells you where to find them in the book.

- *Look at the Pictures*

This book has lots of great photos. Flip through and check out those pictures you like the best. This is a great way to get a quick idea of what this book is all about. Read the captions to learn even more about the photos.

- *Use the Index*

If you are looking for a certain fact, then you might want to turn to the Index at the back of the book. The Index lists the subjects covered in the book. It will tell you what pages to find them on.

▲ A GREAT WHITE SHARK ADVENTURE
If you hire a boat to go shark watching near Cape Town, you
may get to reach out and touch a smiling fellow like this.
Scientists have found that great white sharks like to be touched
on their sensitive snouts. The sharks will stop, relax, and sink
gracefully back into the water.

SOUTH AFRICA'S PAST

South Africa's history is very exciting. It is the story of ancient lands and people, of discovery, of hardship, and of success. Most important, this country's history helped form the South Africa you see today.

Ancient History

Some of the earliest human bones ever found were discovered right in South Africa! Scientists think that these early humans were nomads—people who move from place to place.

Native South Africans and Europeans

Europeans were always curious about South Africa. Some wanted to sail around the southern tip in search of a shortcut to Asia. In 1488, a Portuguese ship went around South Africa's **cape**. Over the next 100 years, many other ships followed this route but nobody wanted to stay in the area. The only people who stayed were seamen stranded in shipwrecks. They met up with two local tribes, the San and the Khoikhoi.

The San and the Khoikhoi tribes were **descendants** of the early African nomads. Early European visitors named them the "bushmen" because they lived in small grass houses in the "bush," an area full of small trees and grasses.

The **trade route** around South Africa's cape (now called the Cape of Good Hope) grew busy with ships. In 1652, the Dutch created a rest stop for ships passing by the cape. These Dutch settlers began farming. This caused a problem with the San and the Khoikhoi, whose land was being taken away.

British Rule

British forces took control of the cape from the Dutch in 1795. Dutch-speaking farmers (called Boers) moved inland and set up towns. The local tribes began to fight for their land. One famous **clan**, the Zulu, whose leader was called Shaka Zulu, was successful in these land wars. Shaka Zulu conquered and united many of the local tribes. He had a large, strong army.

Then, gold and diamonds were discovered. South Africa became well-known and rich. The British began to tighten their control. Wars broke out in **resistance**. They were called the South African Wars.

In 1910, the Union of South Africa became an independent colony of Britain. Yet, South African people were harshly divided along racial lines—Dutch, British, and **native** South Africans who were black. The government reinforced this division by creating a system of **apartheid**—the forced separation of black and white people.

▲ **CASTLE OF GOOD HOPE**
The Castle of Good Hope is located in Cape Town. The first Dutch settlers began building it in 1666. It is the oldest building in South Africa.

From 1948 until 1990, South Africa operated under this policy, keeping blacks and whites **segregated** . In South Africa, skin color determined where people could work, play, live, and even go to school. Black South Africans suffered terribly under apartheid.

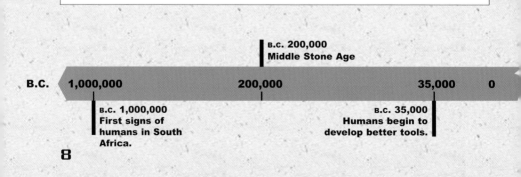

B.C. 200,000
Middle Stone Age

B.C.   1,000,000   200,000   35,000   0

B.C. 1,000,000
First signs of
humans in South
Africa.

B.C. 35,000
Humans begin to
develop better tools.

Laws under apartheid were harsh and controlling. The laws favored the white community and kept black communities in poverty and despair. **Protests** broke out around South Africa calling for equality. Some became violent. Young people who spoke out against apartheid like Stephen Biko were killed. One brave man, Nelson Mandela, was jailed for 28 years for his efforts to end apartheid.

Eventually, the world took notice of these unequal laws. World leaders refused to trade with South Africa unless things changed. It wasn't until 1990 that the South African president F. W. de Klerk ended many of the laws of apartheid. He released Nelson Mandela from prison and lifted the ban on black political organizations.

South Africa Today

Today, people are working to build a better South Africa—where everyone is equal. Signs of this new era are everywhere.

Still, it will take time before the damages of years of inequality are truly erased. In the meantime, South Africans are hopeful about the future.

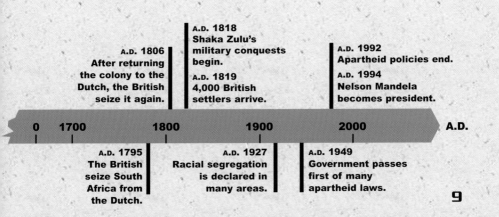

A.D. 1806 After returning the colony to the Dutch, the British seize it again.

A.D. 1818 Shaka Zulu's military conquests begin.

A.D. 1819 4,000 British settlers arrive.

A.D. 1992 Apartheid policies end.

A.D. 1994 Nelson Mandela becomes president.

0   1700   1800   1900   2000   A.D.

A.D. 1795 The British seize South Africa from the Dutch.

A.D. 1927 Racial segregation is declared in many areas.

A.D. 1949 Government passes first of many apartheid laws.

A LOOK AT SOUTH AFRICA'S GEOGRAPHY

South Africa is located at the southernmost tip of the continent of Africa. Early European explorers avoided South Africa because it seemed too great a distance to travel.

Land

There are three major regions of South Africa. Each has a different type of land. There is a large plateau towards the center of the country. It is called the Highveld. A plateau is a large, flat area that is raised higher than the surrounding land. It is covered in grass and lush evergreen trees fed by rainfall from the south.

A ring of mountains surrounds the plateau on all sides. This mountain range is called Drakensberg, or Dragon's Back Mountains. The largest peaks in this range reach higher than 10,000 feet (3,048 meters).

Northern South Africa is mostly desert. Two deserts found in South Africa are the Kalahari and the Namib. The Kalahari Desert is covered in red sands and dry shrubs.

South Africa's savanna is called the Bushveld and is home to several game reserves. As you head south through Little Karoo, a valley within the Great Karoo region, you will see the climate change from hot desert to lush landscape. Little Karoo has plenty of water that runs underground. It is perfect for farming.

SOUTH AFRICA'S SIZE ▶
South Africa looks large, but the map doesn't give a good idea of this country's grandness. South Africa is about 1,000 miles (1,609 km) from north to south and the same distance from east to west.

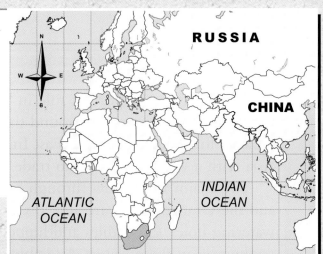

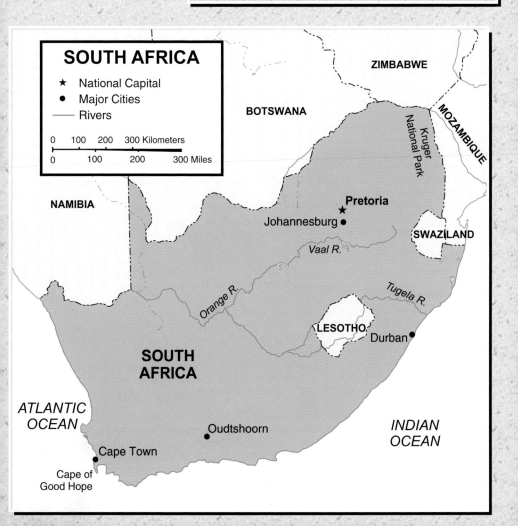

SOUTH AFRICA

★ National Capital
● Major Cities
— Rivers

0   100   200   300 Kilometers
0   100   200   300 Miles

Water

Water plays an important role in South Africa. The first Europeans who sailed around this country were looking for a shortcut to the East Indies, islands near Asia with a wealth of spices to trade.

Two major rivers flow through South Africa, the Vaal and the Orange. There are also lowland streams and watering holes. Crocodiles and hippos can be seen cooling off in these waters. Augrabies Falls National Park is home to one of the biggest waterfalls in the world.

But there is a shortage of drinking water in South Africa. Its desert and dry heat cause this shortage. South Africa has been dealing with this **drought** for years.

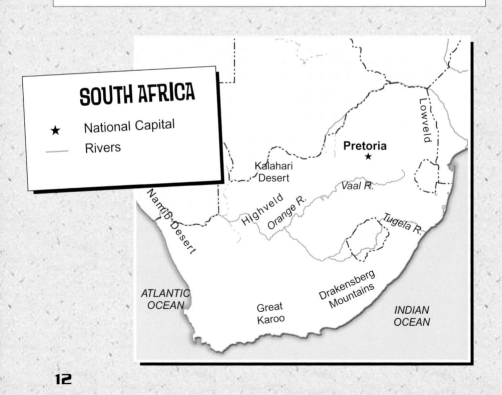

SOUTH AFRICA

★ National Capital

— Rivers

Kalahari Desert

Pretoria ★

Lowveld

Namib Desert

Highveld

Orange R.

Vaal R.

Tugela R.

Drakensberg Mountains

ATLANTIC OCEAN

Great Karoo

INDIAN OCEAN

ORANGE RIVER ▶
The Orange River,
South Africa's
longest, brings
welcome relief
through the desert.

▲ BEAUTIFUL SHORELINES
Swimmers enjoy the calm, clear waters of Boulders
Beach in Cape Peninsula.

◀ **GOOD HOPE FOR SAILORS**
The Cape of Good Hope was the first land that sailors could recognize on their way to South Africa. Its warm weather and beautiful countryside drew many sailors to settle there.

Weather

South Africa is halfway between the **equator** and Antarctica, near the South Pole. That is why in some South African towns, the weather is moderate—not too hot and not too cold. However, in other areas in the country, temperatures can jump all the way up to 120 degrees Fahrenheit (49° C) in the day and dive down to 3 degrees Fahrenheit (-16° C) at night.

Lowland areas get very hot in the summer. But if you head to higher ground in the mountains, you'll be in for a cool treat. The mountain regions often get light rain showers and become covered in fog.

In winter, the mountains may be dusted with a little light snowfall. The northern and western Cape regions are especially lovely in the spring when the wildflowers bloom.

▲ HIGH AND DRY IN THE KALAHARI DESERT
This lizard walks carefully across the hot ground of the Kalahari Desert. The desert is so hot and dry that cracks form in the baked earth.

CAPE TOWN : A BIG-CITY SNAPSHOT

▲ PRETTY CITY
Cape Town is a modern city with many interesting places to
visit. Some call it one of the world's most beautiful cities.

The Main Facts

The Dutch **founded** Cape Town when they arrived in 1652. Now one of the prettiest cities in the world, Cape Town sits on a small **peninsula** at the southern tip of South Africa. Its most famous landmark, Table Mountain, rises above the city. When early European ships sailed around the cape, they looked for Table Mountain—this majestic land mass is visible from 90 miles (145 km) away.

Around Town

Cape Town is one of South Africa's most important business areas. One of the city's first markets, Company's Garden, was located on Adderley Street. It was started in 1652 to provide passing ships with fresh vegetables. Adderley Street is also where you'll find the Old Slave Lodge, built in 1679 to house slaves. Early **seafarers** carved messages into its stones and letters were later left under the looser stones. Today, the Old Slave Lodge displays exhibits like these postal stones, as well as other reminders of the **tragic** times when slaves were kept.

Saint George's Mall and Greenmarket Square are just a short walk from Adderley Street. Street performers are always putting on a show at the Mall. On Greenmarket Square you can visit the Old Town House, a national landmark that was built in 1761. Today, it is home to valuable works of art. From here you can head up to the oldest European building in South Africa, the Castle of Good Hope. It dates back to 1666.

The coast along the cape is great for whale or shark watching and a visit to the Two Oceans Aquarium.

Then, pay a visit to Robben Island, seven miles off the coast. This tiny island was once used as a prison for political prisoners such as Nelson Mandela, who later became South Africa's president. Today, it's a safe home for rare birds. Robben Island also has a lighthouse that was built in 1863.

A good way to get to know Cape Town is to take a stroll down Long Street. It was named in the 1700s and runs straight through the center of town. You can start out on Long Street by the sea and walk until it ends at Table Mountain. You might want to stop at a wonderful souvenir shop called "Junk Shop" and search for unusual treasures like Zulu warrior beads.

Table Mountain

Once you've walked Long Street all the way to Table Mountain, you'll be ready for a break! Rest your feet as you ride the cable car to the top of the mountain. Look out for the mountain's "tablecloth"—white clouds often floating and swirling over the top of the mountain. The clouds cling to the mountaintop like a tablecloth. On the other side of Table Mountain you'll find Cape Flats—the site of Cape Town's smaller, more crowded townships.

The Other Cape

At the end of your visit to Cape Town, you might want to take the short trip to Fanschhoek. This small town lies 50 miles (80 km) out of town and it's where French settlers first lived.

TABLE MOUNTAIN ▶
Rising above the Cape Town waterfront, Table Mountain displays a white "tablecloth" of clouds. A cable car will take you up to the top.

CAPE TOWN'S TOP-10 CHECKLIST

Are you ready for Cape Town? Don't leave before you enjoy these 10 activities.

☐ Stroll through the old center of Cape Town to the top of Adderley Street.

☐ Write a letter and leave it under a loose stone at the Old Slave Lodge.

☐ Walk one block over to watch street performers along Saint George's Mall.

☐ See rare art at Greenmarket Square.

☐ Visit the Castle of Good Hope, the oldest European building in South Africa.

☐ Go whale watching along the coastline.

☐ See delicate underwater animals like crabs and starfish at the Two Oceans Aquarium.

☐ Visit Robben Island, just off the coast of Cape Town.

☐ While on Robben Island, visit the lighthouse, built in 1863.

☐ Take a trip on a cable car to the top of Table Mountain.

4 TOP SIGHTS

South Africa is so large it could take months to see it all, and travel in different parts of South Africa can be difficult. Still, don't leave before you get a chance to visit these great sites.

Oudtshoorn

Diamonds aren't the only riches found in South Africa—ostriches are too! In 1870, ostrich feathers became the biggest fad in Europe. Rich ladies all wanted ostrich feathers to wear in their hats and around their collars. It was the latest fashion trend.

The area around Oudtshoorn proved to be a good place to raise these long-necked birds, and ostrich feather farming proved to be good business. At one point, six feathers from an ostrich sold for over $1,000! Soon, the feather farmers became feather millionaires.

Today, such ridiculous prices are long gone, but ostrich feathers are still in demand. Over 250,000 ostriches live in the Oudtshoorn area. Visit the show farm of Highgate to get up close to these large, flightless birds. There you can pet an ostrich chick or take a ride on an adult, much like you would ride a horse. You can even watch them being plucked!

▼ THE FAST AND THE FLIGHTLESS

The ostrich races at Oudtshoorn draw flocks of tourists. Ostrich feathers are still valuable, so raising these large birds is a big business.

FASCINATING FACT

Ostriches can grow to be more than 8 feet (2.6 m) tall and can weigh up to 300 pounds (135 kg). These big birds lay equally large eggs. Each egg weighs about 3.3 pounds (1.5 kg).

Kruger National Park

No trip to South Africa is complete without a sighting of the "big five"—South Africa's five most popular animals. The big five animals are lions, rhinos, buffalo, leopards, and elephants. They earned this name because they were believed to be the five most dangerous animals. See them for yourself at Kruger National Park.

This park was set up in 1898. It is over 200 miles (322 km) long and up to 50 miles (80 km) wide, making it the largest national park in South Africa. Its great size allows animals to roam freely in their natural **habitat**. Kruger has a great variety of animals, more than any other park in the world. It has 147 **species** of mammals, 512 bird species, and 300 different types of trees.

Most of the land is flat with low hills. Rivers cross through the park. But when there are droughts, the park officials provide water where there is not enough. Most visitors drive through the park to get a view of the animals.

Besides the big five, you can also see giraffes, cheetahs, zebras, and flocks of birds. Though the baboons may beg, please don't feed the animals! (Baboons are monkeys with bright pink bottoms.) When humans feed the animals, the animals begin to depend on humans for food. They forget their natural instincts for finding their own food and surviving in the wild.

▲ HMMM...BANANAS OR NUTS FOR LUNCH?
This baby baboon sits quietly in the shade at Kruger
National Park. Adult baboons are very intelligent,
but they can be dangerous.

Shakaland

Many books and articles have been written about the Zulu people. These writings described them as fierce warriors, making the Zulu culture a favorite subject for movies and novels. While it is true that these warriors fought fiercely to protect their land, the Zulus really were a gentle people.

A popular spot for those in search of Zulu culture is just outside of Eshowe in KwaZulu-Natal. That is where you will find Shakaland. This attraction was once the set created for the television series *Shaka Zulu*. The set was created in 1985. It is no longer in use for filming TV programs, but local dancers still come to use it as a stage.

If you want to see real Zulu warriors, stop by one of the cultural villages around the old set, where you can watch a dance group perform and eat traditional foods. Make sure you take time to purchase some of the Zulu's crafts. The Zulu people are known for being excellent weavers.

◄ WELCOME TO SHAKALAND
This sign welcomes visitors to Shakaland, which was built as a set for the television series Shaka Zulu! Zulu dancers perform there now.

▲ **DRUMBEATS OF SOUTH AFRICA**
A Zulu drummer performs for tourists at Shakaland.
You can learn more about Zulu life and traditions
at the cultural villages nearby.

Gold Reef City

South Africa was always known as one of the best places to find gold. The discovery of gold in the late 1890s started a gold rush near the city of Johannesburg. Gold Reef City is an exact model of a city that existed there in the late 1800s, so if you visit, you will know just how the city looked back then.

The center of Gold Reef City is known as Shaft Number 14. It was started in 1887 by Crown Mines and became the center of the gold mining industry. The mine closed down in 1971 and is now a historic site.

Today, you can take underground tours of the mines. On a tour you can learn how the miners gathered the gold and brought it to the surface to be poured into gold bars.

Walking through the city is like going back in time. There is an old-fashioned hotel, restaurant, and even an amusement park with roller coasters and other rides! Tours can be taken by train or in a horse-drawn carriage. South Africans take pride in this site and show off the local culture with traditional dances and celebrations.

While visiting, you should be sure to see the geological exhibit at Winder House, where you can learn about the surrounding land. There's also a great place to buy some souvenirs like African art, hand-blown glass, and original carvings.

▲ **POURING GOLD**
Gold is heated at very high temperatures until it turns to liquid, and then it is poured into molds for gold bars. The dream of finding gold brought many settlers to South Africa to dig deep in the mines.

GOING TO SCHOOL IN SOUTH AFRICA

In the past, black children were not allowed to go to the same schools as white children. Now, all children go to school together. They start going to school around the age of seven and study English, Afrikaans (the Dutch language), and sometimes native languages. There are 11 official languages spoken in South Africa.

Public schools are very crowded, but the government is trying to change that. South Africans are trying to improve their school system knowing that stronger schools will also make the country stronger.

▲ EQUAL EDUCATION FOR ALL
Students of all races work together in this South African classroom. Years ago, many students fought the old rules of apartheid so today's black and white students can sit side by side.

Most South Africans would agree that soccer is the country's favorite sport. That doesn't mean it's the only sport played there, though. Many kinds of sports are played in South Africa year-round because of the region's warm climate.

Cricket, from England, is another popular sport. It is a game that is similar to baseball but is played with a flat bat. South Africans also enjoy rugby, which is something like football without all the safety pads and with a larger ball.

Long-distance running is also popular in South Africa. In fact, some of the fastest runners in the world are from South Africa, such as Josiah Thugwane. He won a gold medal in the 1996 Olympics for long-distance running.

▲ RUGBY
Many South Africans love the rough sport of rugby, which is played without protective padding and with a ball slightly larger than a football.

FROM FARMING TO FACTORIES

Even though only about 12% of the land in South African can be farmed, that land is known for being rich and fertile, allowing almost anything to be grown. That is why South Africa has so many types of crops, including corn, grain, sugar, fruit, cotton, and tobacco. Many South Africans work at farming these products.

South Africa is also famous for its natural resources. The diamond mines in the town of Kimberely are among the largest in the world. South Africa also produces more gold than anywhere else! There is also coal, iron, nickel, platinum, and copper. Many people work mining, shipping, and shaping these natural resources into finished products.

Tourism is a big business in South Africa. If you visit, you will need to go to the bank and change your money into Rand, the type of money used there. Visitors to South Africa can enjoy seeing wild animals in 15 different game reserves, which offer guided tours and **safaris**. Kruger National Park is one of the most well-known reserves.

Certain times of the year are better for visiting these parks, and the types of animals vary from north to south. Tour guides who know the parks very well usually lead safaris. Some parks can be driven through without any danger, but you will want a guide who knows where the hippos are bathing and the lions are resting. Bring your camera and lots of film!

A FORTUNE IN DIAMONDS ▶
Many of the world's diamonds are mined in South Africa. They are used not only in jewelry but also in industry—diamonds are so hard that they can be used to cut other stones.

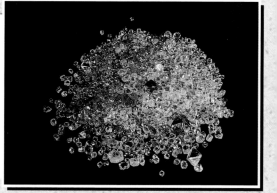

▼ ON SAFARI
These tourists on a photo safari are getting their money's worth! Tourism is an important business in South Africa. People come from all over the world to see animals like this great elephant in the wild.

31

THE SOUTH AFRICAN GOVERNMENT

Over the years, South Africa has had many names. Now it is officially called the Republic of South Africa. A republic means that the citizens are allowed to vote for their lawmakers and their president.

The government of South Africa was once led by the all-white National Party (NP). It was the main political party in South Africa even though most South Africans were black. The NP controlled the government from 1948 to 1994. This party kept up a policy of apartheid. The largest black political party is the African National Congress (ANC). It was formed in 1912. This group was against apartheid and its leaders were put in jail because they wanted power to be shared.

In 1994, the ANC took the majority of the votes. Nelson Mandela became president of South Africa. One of the things that happened under ANC leadership was the creation of a new constitution. It guarantees the equality of men and women no matter what their race or beliefs.

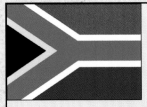

SOUTH AFRICA'S NATIONAL FLAG

The South African flag represents all of the different groups that live in this country. The six colors on the flag stand for the union between Zulus, Afrikaners, Muslims, and other groups of all colors living there. The "Y" in the center symbolizes a divided road becoming a unified one.

RELIGIONS OF SOUTH AFRICA

South Africa is a land of many colors, just like its flag. That means there are many different types of people and religions. Today the major religions in South Africa are Christianity, Hinduism, Islam, and Judaism.

The religious practices of South Africa have been through changes over the years. The original tribal peoples believed that a supreme being created Earth. They also believed that their dead ancestors watched over them. Religions of the Khoi San, the Zulu, and the Xhosa tribes all had rituals and myths that were used to ask favors of the dead, and traditional folktales helped people to live better.

Christian and Muslim **missionaries** helped **convert** many of the tribal people. However, traditional South African religions still play a part in daily life. Herd boys in South Africa still use praying mantises (insects) to "pray" for their lost animals.

PORT ELIZABETH SYNAGOGUE ▶
A synagogue is where Jewish people gather for religious services. The words in Hebrew welcome Jews to prayer. There is a large Jewish population in South Africa.

SOUTH AFRICAN FOOD

South Africa is a mix of different cultures—and so is its food. British and Dutch foods are easily found there. Native foods often use similar ingredients, like corn and grains, but the food tastes very different.

Other cultures have left their mark on South African cuisine. Indian curries and other spices flavor many dishes. Seafood is popular, too, because South Africa's two oceans are filled with sea life.

One traditional treat is called the "potjie." This is sort of a twist on the traditional barbecue. The women get together around a huge three-legged cast iron pot to cook the meals. They put all their ingredients into a pot and place it over hot coals. Meanwhile, the men prepare a huge fire for the barbecue. The potjie is an all-day party and anything can be cooked this way. One popular dish is called ostrich potjie, made with ostrich meat. Many other different kinds of meat are also used.

South African mealie-meal is also a popular dish. Mealie-meal is a stiff, steamed porridge made from white corn flour and served with stews or roasted meat, fish, or vegetables. Will you take some mealie-meal with your ostrich potjie?

◀ **DRIED OSTRICH MEAT...NOT YOUR EVERYDAY TREAT!**
Many of the ostriches raised in South Africa are used for meat. While you're there, be bold and try some.

South Africa's Recipe

BOBOTIE

Ingredients:

1 1/2 cups milk

3 slices day-old bread

2 eggs

2 medium onions, chopped

1 garlic clove, minced

1/2 cup slivered almonds

1/2 cup raisins

1 tbsp sugar

1 tbsp salt

1 tsp curry powder

1/8 tsp pepper

1 tsp vinegar

1 tsp lemon juice

1 1/2 lbs. ground beef or lamb, or a mixture.

WARNING:

Never cook or bake by yourself. Always have an adult assist you in the kitchen.

Directions:

Preheat oven to 350 degrees Fahrenheit. Soak the bread slices in milk. Squeeze the extra milk from bread into a bowl and set the milk to the side. Combine all the ingredients, except for the milk and one egg. Press this mixture into an 11 x 7 inch baking dish. Add enough milk to the milk that was set aside to make 3/4 cup. Beat the egg and milk together and pour this over the mixture. Bake, uncovered, for one hour or until golden brown and firm to the touch.

UP CLOSE: THE GARDEN ROUTE

The long distance between the Slang and Storms Rivers is known as the Garden Route. This trail is named for its beautiful plant and animal life. Along the Garden Route, you can see everything from a tropical forest to wild hippos.

The Garden Route is a popular ecotourist hot spot. Ecotourists are people who go on vacations that are safe for the environment. That means no fancy hotels and no disturbing the wildlife or their habitat.

There are several ways to experience the Garden Route so it's best to have a guide or a good plan. Toward the north, the route begins on a high mountain range. From this point there are many different trails that take you down the coastline with many coves, bays, and beaches to explore. Now is your chance to go whale watching. Whale watching is very popular. Visitors go out on boats or watch from the shore with binoculars to see the huge, gentle whales swim or leap above the ocean. Tourists come from all over the world to see the great white sharks that live in South African waters. (Most of these are found near Cape Town.) South African great white sharks are famous for jumping high out of the water to catch seals. You won't find great whites do this anywhere else in the world!

▲ OCEAN VIEW ALONG THE GARDEN ROUTE
These homes have a wonderful view of the sea and
of the beautiful Garden Route in South Africa.

▲ CANGO CAVES
Visitors enjoy looking at stalactites in the Cango Caves, located on the Garden Route. Stalactites are the sharp rocks that point down from the top of the caves.

The town of George is known as "the Gateway to the Garden Route." George sits at the foot of Outeniqua Mountain. It is surrounded by thick, green plant life. From here you might start by visiting an ostrich farm or preparing to photograph wildlife. Then, along the Garden Route you'll find many places to go scuba diving. You might even try kayaking, where you can paddle along in a small boat large enough for only one or two people.

This journey will bring you to some of the most amazing natural sights in the world. With planning, visitors can climb mountains, hike through deep forests, and then do a little fishing along the coast.

CAPE PROVINCE COASTLINE ▶
The Garden Route offers so many pretty sights, you'll never want to put your camera down.

HOLIDAYS

South Africans celebrate more national holidays than most other countries in the world. Many of these holidays celebrate equal rights and the end of apartheid.

Freedom Day, on April 27, is one of these times. It commemorates the day in 1994 when people of all races and colors could vote in the first democratic elections.

Youth Day is an important holiday. It honors the students who rioted to protest apartheid in the schools. There is a memorial service in the morning. The world-famous Comrads Marathon is run on this day also. May 1 is Workers' Day, or May Day. It honors people who work in all types of jobs. Most people have the day off of school or work. There are often many parades.

The Day of Reconciliation on December 16 is a two-part holiday in South Africa. Afrikaners started celebrating it to remember the day in 1838 when a Zulu

army was defeated. Activists in the African National Congress celebrate the beginning of when they began to overthrow apartheid.

▲ **HOLIDAY PARADE**
Musicians perform in a holiday parade celebrating the end of apartheid and the birth of a government for all of the people.

LEARNING THE LANGUAGE

English	Zulu	How to say it
Good day; "I see you"	Sawubona	SOW–BOW–na
How are you?	Ninjani	nin–JAH–nee
Thank you	Ngiyabonga	NN–GEE–ya–BOON–ga
Go well	Hambe kahle	HAM–ba GOSH–lee
Stay well	Sale kahle	SAH–lay GOSH–lee
We are learning	Siyafunda	see–ya–FOON–da

PASOP VIR BOBBEJANE
BEWARE OF BABOONS

QUICK FACTS

SOUTH AFRICA

Capital ▶
Cape Town (legislative)
Pretoria (administrative)
Bloemfontein (judicial)

Borders
Botswana (N)
Mozambique (NE)
Namibia (W)
Swaziland (NE)
Zimbabwe (NE)
Lesotho (Within eastern
South Africa)

Area
471,008 square miles
(1,219,912 sq km)

Population
43,647,658

▼ **Main Religious Groups**

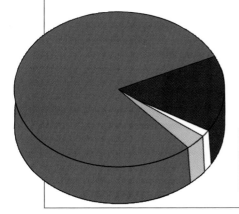

Largest Cities
Johannesburg (5,700,000 people)
Cape Town Peninsula (2,350,157)
East Rand (1,378,792)
Durban/Pinetown (1,137,378)
Pretoria (1,080,187)

Chief Crops
Corn, wheat, sugarcane,
fruits, vegetables, beef,
poultry, mutton, wool,
dairy products

■ Christians 68%
▨ Muslim 2%
☐ Hindu 1.5%
■ Other 28.5%

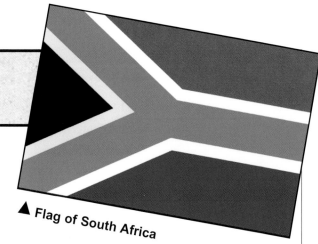

▲ Flag of South Africa

Longest River
Orange River
1,300 miles (2,100 km)

Coastline ▶
1,739 miles (2,798 km)

Literacy Rate
82% of all South Africans
can read

Major Industries
Mining (world's largest
producer of platinum,
gold, and chromium),
automobile assembly,
metalworking, machinery,
textile, iron and steel,
chemicals, fertilizer,
foodstuffs

Natural Resources
Gold, chromium,
antimony, coal, iron ore,
manganese, nickel,
phosphates, tin, uranium,
gem diamonds, platinum,
copper, vanadium, salt,
natural gas

◀ **Monetary Unit**
Rand

PEOPLE TO KNOW

◀ DESMOND TUTU

Desmond Tutu became the first black secretary general of the South African Council of Churches, which represents 12 million Christians. In 1984, he became the first black bishop of Johannesburg and was awarded the Nobel Peace Prize. He is very outspoken and has fought for equal rights for all, winning the hearts of South Africans of all colors.

NELSON MANDELA ▶

Nelson Mandela is one of the most famous people of South Africa. When he was young, Mandela spoke out against the treatment of black people during apartheid. He was sentenced to life in prison for his speeches in 1962. Finally in 1990, he was freed—after 28 years in jail! Nelson Mandela became president of South Africa in 1994.

◀ LAURENCE OWEN GANDER

Laurence Owen Vine Gander was an important newspaper editor. He wrote anti-apartheid articles in 1965 that revealed the horrible conditions black people lived under in South Africa. His reports helped to end people's apartheid and to allow true majority rule.

MORE TO READ

Do you want to know more about South Africa? Check out the books below.

Fish, Bruce. *South Africa: 1880 to the Present: Imperialism, Nationalism, and Apartheid (Exploration of Africa: The Emerging Nations).* Chelsea House Publishing, 2000.
South Africa's rich history comes to life in this comprehensive look into the country's politics and culture.

Frankel, Glenn. *Rivonia's Children: Three Families and the Cost of Conscience in White South Africa.* Continuum Publishing, 2001.
Understand the story behind the Rivonia Trial, which sent Nelson Mandela and many of his Jewish supporters to jail.

McKee, Tim. *No More Strangers Now: Young Voices from a New South Africa.* DK Publishing, 2000.
Read real-life stories of how a teenager raised during apartheid overcame racism.

Woodhouse, Jane. *Nelson Mandela (Lives and Times).* Heinemann, 1998.
Follow this pictorial journey through Nelson Mandela's life and experiences.

GLOSSARY

Apartheid (uh-PART-hite)—the official policy of racial segregation in South Africa

Cape (KAPE)—a large, pointed piece of land that is mostly surrounded by ocean

Clan (KLAN)—a family group that includes aunts, uncles, cousins, and many generations

Convert (kuhn-VERT)—to change beliefs or behavior

Descendants (dih-SEN-duhnts)—the children and grandchildren of a group or person

Drought (DROWT)—a period of very dry weather that may result in crop failures and deaths of animals and people

Equator (eh-KWAY-ter)—an invisible line around the Earth, halfway between the North and South Poles

Founded (FOWN-ded)—set up a business, a town, or a country

Habitat (HAB-ih-tat)—the natural area in which an animal or plant lives

Missionaries (MIH-shuhn-air-eez)—people sent by a church to another country to tell the people there about their church's beliefs

Native (NAY-tihv)—belonging to the first people who lived in a place

Peninsula (pen-IN-soo-lah)—a long piece of land surrounded mainly by water

Protests (PROW-tests)—demonstrations or displays against something

Resistance (reh-ZISS-tuhnce)—fighting against an unwelcome ruler

Safaris (suh-FAR-eez)—a trip people take to see, photograph, or hunt wild animals

Seafarers (SEE-fair-erz)—sailors, fishermen, and others who travel on the seas

Segregated (SEHG-ruh-gay-ted)—separated into groups. People have often been segregated by their skin color, leading to unequal treatment.

Species (SPEE-sheez)—one kind of animal or plant

Trade route (TRAYD root)—the path across land or sea taken by travelers from many countries so they can buy things from each other

Tragic (TRAD-jeh-dee)—unpleasant or extremely sad. Often refers to a situation, like segregation.

INDEX